Most of us constantly seek something other than what is—a better job or more degrees, better abs or a more perfect partner. In his simple way, *Kosho the Toad* lights up another path for us. With all his warts, humor and love of hard liquor, he keeps his little body aimed at *awakening*. Like a bent old monk writing on a cave wall, he hops along and points out what he sees, simply and honestly. I'll delightedly read him to my son, to Zen students, and on a barely-light morning, to a blank wall.

~ Sara Jisho Siebert, Soto Zen Priest, Ames, Iowa

Other Books by Robert Tremmel:

Driving the Milford Blacktop: Poems (BkMk Press)

There is a Naked Man: Poems (Main Street Rag)

Crossing Crocker Township: Poems (Timberline Press)

Zen and the Practice of Teaching English, with William J. Broz
(Heinemann-Boynton/Cook)

Teaching Writing Teachers (Heinemann-Boynton/Cook)

Bottom Dog Press

The Records
of Kosho the Toad

Robert Tremmel

Those who accept words are lost;
those who linger in phrases are deluded.

—John Daido Loori

Laughing Buddha Series
Bottom Dog Press
Huron, Ohio

Bottom Dog Press, Inc.
PO Box 425, Huron, OH 44839
Lsmithdog@aol.com
http://smithdocs.net

Credits:
General Editor and Layout Design: Larry Smith
Cover Design: Susanna Sharp-Schwacke
Author Photo: Michelle Peters Tremmel

Acknowledgments

"Toad Story," "Hearing," and "Eight More Oxherding Pictures in Search of Drawings" were published in *Cloudbank*. Thanks to the editor, Michael Malan, for his encouragement and support.

Contents

AUTHOR'S NOTE

What follows is based on the records of a toad's life. Although much has been changed for this accounting, it must be regarded as a true record. However, it should in no way be considered as an orthodox representation or adequate response to the *Blue Cliff Record,* a text upon which some of the records are based.

Likewise, these records should not be understood to be an orthodox interpretation of the last two thousand years of Christian thought or practice. It's not very accurate on toads either.

Part 1

The Short Trip

If you go on wandering around, you won't ever
be able to find the road.

Blue Cliff Record Case 24

TOAD STORY

A toad hops into a bar.

Could be any bar
and Kosho any toad.

He orders Glendronach
straight up in a snifter.

By the time
he reaches for his glass
he is already an old toad
and the bar is empty
except for the bartender
and a young man
with a bluegreen lacquer bucket
mopping the floor in front
of the men's room, a fresh
bouquet of flowers blooming
in a blue vase
on a single table
next to the window, the road
outside the window
like a river running
down to the sea and Kosho.

DREAM

Kosho dreams he is a tall
blond-haired man, dressed
in a dark suit, with a red
power tie, gold cuff links
and carrying a brief case
through a revolving door.

Once inside, he sees
a wide stair winding up
between a waterfall
on the right and sunny
windows on the left.

The last thing
he remembers
before waking
is the color
of the carpet—white

and how bright red
the blood stains on it are.

BODY

No matter what
he might have dreamed
Kosho's body is still
the body of an old toad

saggy, with wrinkled
skin, bulging eyes
and a lower lip
that droops like the rim
of a pitcher.

One knee hurts
when he bends it
and his left hip
stiffens when he sits.

When he hops slowly
to work, those around him
make room, open doors
and call him *sir*.

LEAVES

Kosho limps
through leaves
in his backyard.

It is barely
October, yet
they are already
up to his knees
and getting deeper
by the moment.

He wonders where
they are coming from
since he lives
on an open plain
and the only trees
are miles away
along the river
and the only
real wind
he has ever felt
in this place
flows from the gift
and the burden
of his own breathing.

PRAYER

Kosho the toad
hops into church, dips
his fingers in holy
water, crosses himself
and kneels to pray.

His prayer lasts
a long time, many kalpas
and in it he prays
for all toads, living
and dead, for the oppressors
of toads, winged, wriggling, four
legged, legless, two
legged, slithering, axe-
wielding, stabbing, rock
throwing, chemical
spraying mass murderers
and their mothers.

He prays for the rich
that they might imagine
the poor, and the poor
that they might have compassion
for the rich.

He prays for the sick
that they might become well
and the well that they might become
sick and the circles
become closed.

He prays that the church might rock
on its foundations, the walls

around him crack and crumble
into dust and the memory
of dust and the sky clear
and the sun shine
on a perfectly flat
treeless plain, a smooth
gleaming planet with no
blemish or stain, where no
prayer is ever uttered
and all questions
have the same answer.

FLIES

Kosho the toad
goes down to the river
to pray, down
to the river, down
to the river to pray.

The flies
gather there with him, cross
all their legs, sit
on his back, his tongue

clear their eyes

and chant the Sutra
of All Meat
Living and Dead
and the Mantra
of Crossing Over
to the Other Side.

gate, gate

paragate

parasamgate

ite missa est.

POSTURE

In the zendo
Kosho lights incense
in the dark morning
of late fall.

Wind from the high plains
moans and descends
as he sits, crosses
his legs, tips
his pelvis forward, folds
one hand into the other
and rests his tongue
against the roof
of his mouth.

His lower lip droops
even more
and the skin loosens
across his chin.

Kosho can't remember
who taught him to sit
like this, but with winter
so near, and spring
following right after
this is the only posture
that makes
any sense at all.

Hearing

Kosho the toad sits
in the church, trying
to hear the priest talk.

Even though his mouth
moves and his hands
make meaningful gestures
in the air, no sound
seems to be coming forth.

Kosho thinks this must be
the result of some strange
quirk of toad evolution.

All the people sitting
around him seem
to be hearing something
and every once in awhile
even the small child
eating cheerios
and coloring dinosaurs
pauses and pays attention.

The mass servers sit
in deep attention
wearing white cassocks
with wooden crosses
dangling from leather cords.

Jesus hangs on his wooden cross
but neither He nor Kosho
can hear one blessed word.

MYSTERIES

Kosho tips forward
onto the kneeler
like a cushion.

So simple.

Below him, in front
of the altar
the coffin lid is closed.

All the scent in the room
is cut off, sputtering
wax and acrid
wick, incense, sharp
blades of perfume
and the rotting
breath of flowers.

Kosho wonders
whose hands these are
folded on his chest.

He shifts his weight
from one knee
to the other.

Whose knees these are
is a mystery as well.

EMPTY

Except for the gruesome
scenes hanging on the wall
and the hopeful dreams
arranged in colored glass
the sanctuary
is empty
and finally at peace.

All the singers are gone
and their songs gone with them.

Green veins pulse
at the heart
of marble, fade
into the shadows
behind it, and the shadows
within those.

The priest is gone.

Kosho the toad is gone.

The dry air
behind the heavy
brass door at the center
of the universe waits
for someone
or something
to breathe it in.

DOKUSAN

The moment he sees Kosho
the Zen Master draws
a circle in the dust
gathered on the floor.

Immediately, Kosho
turns around and leaves.

The Zen Master gets up
and closes the door.

Kosho's footprints
in the dust are erased
by the hem
on the Master's robe

RIVERS

Kosho packs his bag
for a short trip, shirts
in one place, pants
in another

some little toad snacks
and a bottle of vodka.

Even though he knows
where he is going
he has no idea
where he will end up
or if he will ever return.

From his front door
the road rises
to the west, bridges shine
in the sun, passing
over muddy rivers
that dig at the earth
like carrion birds

Missouri, Platte, Colorado

Rio Grande

the broken bodies
of men, of women
and toads alike
wash up on the banks
and sand bars

and faraway mountains
are already awake
and walking to meet him.

Highway 159

Kosho follows
the road that flows
across the high desert

all around him
the blood of Christ flows
across the land

and through him
also it flows.

Bosque

Kosho hops down a trail
through cottonwood bottoms
to the edge of the river.

The water flows there
like a mountain stream
but churns with mud
the color of flesh
and the bodies
that float just
beneath the surface

WONDER

In the chapel
along the road, Kosho
the toad crosses
his legs again, feels
his spine straighten
and only then
does he wonder
if he closed the windows
of his truck, pushed
the refrigerator door
all the way shut
before he left his house
and what he will eat
for dinner next Tuesday.

GIFT

Kosho tips slowly
along a mountain
trail through a wide
stand of wild roses.

From time to time he stops
just to savor
the subtle, spicy scent
and study the patches
of snow on the peaks
above the valley
he is moving through.

Up there, Kosho knows all
too well, tiny flowers
grow from solid rock
in a shallow space, no
deeper than the covers
on his bed, and there is no
scent, just breathing
in the light
and breathing color out.

HOUSEKEEPING

Back home
Kosho moves from room
to room, adjusting windows
the way a sailor
might adjust the sails

raising some to catch
more wind, lowering some
to release the wind
and the sound of the wind

and at each window
he prays a silent
gatha, that he might
raise it with his full
attention and lower it
with respect for the wood
and where it comes from

for the glass and the fire
it went through

for the screen beyond
and its vigilance.

STILL BODY

As it was before
Kosho's body is still
the body of an old toad

with the same thick, saggy
and wrinkled skin, the same
red eyes and drooping lip.

His knee still hurts
and his hip still stiffens
when he sits, and still
the flat land
all around him
carries him
as still water
receives the moon.

Equinox

Kosho the toad lies
awake in his toad bed.

It is 3 A.M.
and even the soft, down-
filled pillows seem hard
as living rock
and dull pain crawls
all over his head
and through his ears
deep into his mind
where the fear always waits.

Outside, he can hear
a cold rain washing
down his window, washing
summer away, washing
sleep away, floating him
on a tide of pain
as he breathes
each breath in, each
breath out and opens
his hands and floats on
toward the other shore
with his pain and his fear
safely stowed on board.

COLLECTION

Kosho sits back
in the pew, not yet
ready to kneel.

He watches
the collection basket
roll his way like a wave
on a warm afternoon
and when it arrives
he floats it
on his fingertips
and passes it on

relieved and grateful
for this chance
to come so close
to touching others
and being touched

to join again
in the weaving
of lives around him
without getting caught
or tangled up or thrown
off just yet into the vast
and beautiful
emptiness hanging
at the front
of the church, just
beyond everyone's reach.

Auction

Kosho stands in the cool mist
at the end of a cloudy
October day.

An auctioneer is up
on a flatbed trailer
trying to sell a box
of broken dishes
or rocks.

On the lawn all around
a dead man's life
is spread out
and covered with mist

dressers, chairs, chainsaws, book
shelves, rakes, hoses, a live
trap large enough for a coon
all covered with mist.

Tools are stacked
under the eave
of the garage, and inside
guns are lined up
on a long table

Beretta twenty-gauge
automatic, Ruger
.22, Stevens side-
by-side, Winchester
.30-30, and a crowd
of men packed in
around them like shad

pushed up against the bank
by October wind.

The mist becomes
the rain, the rain becomes
the dark and to save himself
Kosho melts
into the long, cool grass.

PAIN

Kosho has a pain deep
in his gut, and nothing
he can do
will make it go away.

If he eats, the pain is there.

If he fasts, the pain is there.

If he prays, pain.

If he curses, still pain.

Kosho and his pain
go everywhere together
and stay home together.

Each leaf
in the plum thicket
falls into the world
of Kosho's pain

remnants of fog
left over from last night
trail away like smoke

the sun shines

so beautiful, so
blessed, so
burdened with pain.

GUESSING

Kosho is up in the night
again.

This time, a sudden
dizziness washes
over him, and to stay
conscious he drops down
and presses his forehead
against the floor
and raises his palms.

When the worst passes
he crawls across the hall
back to his room and lifts
his body back into bed.

The room is dark, thinning
leaves on the vines
outside the window
block the bright lights
that rise with the night.

Soon, all those leaves will be gone
and the frightening shadows
and shafts of light piercing
the blinds will make
Kosho wonder
whether he is awake
or asleep, living
or dying
or all of these, or none.

FALL

Kosho the toad studies
a petal just fallen
from a stem
he has never seen.

It is deep red, supple
as skin with pulsing veins.

Kosho turns to the pile
of books and computers
on the table
and scans text after text
for word about this petal
and why it exists.

But no luck.

He even tries talking
to the petal, asking
questions, but the petal
remains silent

the statue of a saint
or the inside
of a chalice.

THEOLOGY

Kosho the toad slides
his boat across
the flat October water

a feather, already
blowing across ice.

Pelicans are bunched up
along the bank, wise
old Franciscans
shitting and working
in secret to undermine
the complacent
hierarchy of the sand.

Wedges of geese
pour down from the north.

Kosho smells the terror
of shad in the water
all around him and hears
the cries of gulls.

SAND

Kosho the toad wakes
in the early morning
from a long
disturbed sleep, out
of sorts and out
of balance, with sharp
edges of bone protruding
through his skin
and fire in every joint.

He begins pacing back
and forth, back and forth
in his bedroom
and then moves outside
to pace in his yard
and deepen the groove
he has already worn
between the sage
and the mulch pile.

Finally, in frustration
he goes down
to his workshop, takes
a piece of sandpaper
and begins to sand the sharp
edges on his shoulders
and then his elbows, hips
and knees, praying
as he sands for the smooth
polished surface of peace
and then he reaches
for the finest grain

to begin sanding
the rough spots that always
seem to appear
in the confused
and unsettled matter
behind his eyes.

EDGE

In the complete
cloudy darkness of night
Kosho the toad moves
through a crushing tangle
of multifora rose
and berry vines

his feet crunch across
the needles and the thorns

and after a while, he can't
even tell what
is up, what
is down and where
the sheer edge
he knows is nearby
might be

although he does remember
reading one time
that he would not
be able to understand it
anyway, *because*
the only people
who really know
where it is are the ones
who have gone over.

FEBRUARY

Kosho drives home
after another
day of work

his hands sag
on the steering wheel

his feet sag on the pedals

his face sags behind his face.

Off to the right, across
a deep, flat expanse
of fields packed
with ice and snow
a giant red ovum drops
through the horizon

the fields are on fire

the ice is on fire

Kosho is on fire.

SHOPPING

Kosho wheels his cart
up and down the wide
aisles of the grocery store.

He is so overwhelmed
by the bewildering
array of items
on the shelves, riot
of colors, blaring
labels, he begins
to run and his palms
get sweaty and slide
on the handle of his cart.

After what seems like hours
of panic he comes to rest
in front of a fresh
meat and fish case
and turns to his brothers
and sisters resting there.

A wing whispers to him
beyond the range of hearing
and says, *when a bird flies by*
feathers fall.

A salmon with a wide
creased brow adds
when a fish swims through
the water is muddied

remember the poor.

A disembodied
liver sings
the ultimate path
is without difficulty

just avoid picking
and choosing

just this

and you can't learn this just once.

PRESSURE

Kosho the toad
sweats and strains
under the weight
of the whole sky and
earth gravity black.

His arms are too heavy
to lift, his knees
dead stone pressed
into the ground, his guts
are flattened
against his bones.

From where he is stuck
Kosho can see a wide
expanse of water, cool
and shimmering, eager
for him to wade in and sink
down far enough
so it can crush him.

TOAD NATURE

Kosho mourns
in the lonely
untouched silence
of poison flowing
from his skin
and the glands
behind his ears
and the sudden
awareness
that he cannot
move an inch
and there is nowhere
for him to go
from here
and no there
where he can arrive.

Interlink

There is no gate from the beginning,
so how do you pass through it?

Wu-Men

EIGHT MORE OXHERDING PICTURES
IN SEARCH OF DRAWINGS

1. Living free and unbothered by the concerns of humans.

Alone and settled in the deep, cool forest
　I graze untroubled and without worries
far from the world of gain and loss
　nameless and settled in mind and body.

2. Sensing Shithead rummaging through the underbrush.

But even this garden of peace and contentment
　is part of the restless world.
No matter how far away heaven may seem
　it cannot be far enough.

3. First glimpse of Shithead.

A single rabbit gives birth to endless troubles.
　At the edge of what was an empty clearing
the bushes and lower branches shake and give way
　and confusion stumbles in.

4. Being caught by Shithead.

There was no need for him to come this far.
   Everything he needed for the rest of his life
he left at home, where even now
   thieves are stealing his laundry and drinking his
Scotch.

5. Humoring Shithead.

Even though he seems sure of himself
   he handles the rope as if it were a snake.
The sooner he thinks he has me
   the sooner his delusion will free me.

6. Letting Shithead have his day.

Riding on my back and tooting his flute
   he is a victorious general
waving to other stragglers along the road
   who also show him compassion and cheer.

7. Leaving Shithead to his own resources.

He believes what he dreams, his house crumbles
    and weeds grow up in his fields.
All the tracks in the earth, sky, and water
    lead away from this sad and needless ruin.

8. Back in the forest.

A light breeze blows through the leaves
    and branches sway lazily in the sun.
Once again I am home, grazing secretly within
    where red flowers naturally bloom red.

Part 2

The Long Trip

The toad in the snow catches and swallows the tiger.

Kusan Sunim

THE HOLY TRUTHS ARE EMPTY

As soon as Kosho the toad
arrives he goes
to be examined
by the driver's license
examiner, takes
a number and sits down
to wait his turn.

When zero appears
on the video screen
Kosho goes up
to the window with zero
posted above it
and waits to be examined.

Who is facing me?
the man at the window asks.

I don't know, Kosho replies
but the man
does not understand
so he turns to the woman
at window number one
and asks, *Who is this toad?*

I don't know
the woman replies
so the man types *I don't know*
into the blank, and after that
Kosho leaves, crosses
the river and arrives

where he sits down
all by himself.

Years later, he is still
sitting with his number
in his pocket
and waiting for the blank space
at the center
of his body to be
filled in or left as it is.

SICKNESS

Kosho's sickness still
creeps sometimes
across the clock face
like a toad, full
of poison and looking
for a place to hide.

In the day, the sun turns
the whole land
into desert

at night, the icy moon
moves tides that erase
the sand and then pulls
them back again.

In the Blue Dragon's cave
the fire is hot, the pain
pearl smooth.

CAKES

Kosho walks through the dust
down an empty road
with his precious books
and everything he owns
riding on his back
and in the shade
of an over-hanging tree
he meets an old woman
selling fried cakes.

The cakes are light
golden brown, dripping
with oil and smell
like the breath of heaven.

The old woman says to Kosho
If you lay down your burden
here, at this side of the road
for only one moment
I will give you all
the fried cakes you can eat.

Kosho looks east
then west, shrugs his shoulders
and continues on down
the road, with his empty
teacup rattling
against his knife, his guts
growling, his mind pacing
like a toothless lion
in a cage, the weight
of all the books

in his pack, his whole house
heavy on his back
and the next woman
selling cakes still
miles on down the road.

IMMERSION

Kosho the toad moves
from one Station
of the Cross
to the next, kneeling
in front of each one
until his knees crack
on the marble floor.

Even if he would
have had eyebrows
to begin with
they would have fallen out
long ago.

A persistent fly
circles his head
and tries to land
in his eyes

but still, the tiger
cannot enter the mountain.

Down in front
a blue-eyed foreigner
with only one shoe
sips the water
at the baptismal font
and then washes his dusty foot.

In-Between

Kosho keeps moving down
the road, still carrying
his burden like his own
body on his back.

Somewhere, far out ahead
in the mountain
a turtle-nosed snake waits
to catch Kosho's scent.

The ass he passed on the road
years ago recedes
into the distance.

The hoofmarks of the horse
and the hound
he is following after
fade on the edge of the road.

Heavy-headed cattle
in the fields on either side
disappear like turtle doves
into mist

ponies run wild through tall
green grass down
to the edge of the sea.

RYUMONJI

Kosho spins down
rapids, straining
to stay afloat
like a dry leaf caught
in autumn wind

cloudy water churns
beneath him, cloudy
sky churns above, sparks flash
on the stones and crashing
cataracts of fire
like arrow points meeting.

Silent blue mountains
pass by unseen, hidden
valleys open like blossoms

fish sprout wings
and sail away
without effort.

IMPASSE

Part I

Kosho the toad races
down city streets
and feels the hot breath
of the tiger on his ass.

All the warts and poison glands
on his body are pumping
thick streams
with the unmistakable scent
of unmanageable fear.

At last he turns
into an alley and flies
down the narrow way
past blank back doors
and garbage dumpsters
to a solid concrete wall
and stops.

Part II

Kosho the toad returns
from the darkness
at the end of the alley
and rides into a bar
on the tiger's head
carrying a sword.

He smells sweet as lilacs
in April and far
from the demons of fear.

The bartender
is surprised to see him
and the two professors
over in the corner
with dragon heads and snake tails
breathe deeply and interrupt
their shouting and cursing
in order to watch something
neither one understands
and will not remember
in the morning.

The Blue Cliff Record

Kosho labors
over the old text
like a monkey
in a hall of mirrors
and as he turns each page
it crumbles
on his desk.

Finally, all he has left
are two faded
covers, a pile of blue dust
and the golden raven
that flies by day
and the jade rabbit
that runs through the sky at night.

CONSUMMATION

Kosho sits
facing the wall
while the wind
blows, seasons
turn, grasses
on the prairie
sprout green, ripen
under the sun
and sow
their seeds.

Even though
he does not
notice it
at some point
his legs turn
to dust, his skin
sags away
from his bones
and the grindstone
of his own mind
wears him down
to a fine edge
then grinds the edge
the way water
grinds away rock
and fire
consumes the host.

VOYAGE

One day, Kosho the toad
returns to the river, flows
all the way
to the sea, then drifts
for years beneath the surface
breathing through the warts
on his back and living
on salt and seaweed
until one day he floats
to the top, just as a board
with a toad-sized hole
in the center appears
overhead, and up
Kosho pops and crawls
out of the water
onto the board
which bears him
lightly as the tip
of a single hair
would carry a lion.

FINDING THE ROAD

All day Kosho packs
his bags, carefully
weighing and measuring
each item, mindfully
placing each
in its proper place.

When he finishes
he places his bags
at the door, lays
his itinerary
on top and takes
the long way
to bed.

Six months later
he takes the same way back
to the door, dusts off
his bags, carefully
unpacks them and places
his itinerary
in the scrap book
of his travels.

JOINTS

Kosho the toad finally
comes to where the last
Station of the Cross
is bolted to the wall
and kneels on the stone floor.

Light streams down
from skylights, stained glass
parses the morning sun
into shepherds and robes

and then the image before him
like all the others, fades
into Kosho's eyes
and the rough brickwork
behind the painted plaster
reappears, the joints
between the bricks crumble
into sand and cement
and the bricks themselves
return to dust.

POINT OF DEPARTURE

Kosho sits in the back
far corner of the church
where he is always
nearly the last
to receive the Eucharist
but he hears the Priest's words clearly
as if they were his mother's
and whispered in his ear.

Even though you
have cobbled together
this creature with your name
its body will return
to earth, its blood
to water, its breath
to fire, its movement
to wind, its mind
to where it came from.

And at this very point
Kosho understands, rises
from his seat, bows deeply
and leaves alone
through a side door
beneath an inscription
fading into the plaster:

Through each gate
there is a road
empty and desolate.

THE DUST SETTLES

Each chapter
of Kosho's story
is exactly the same
as the chapter before

first the confusion
then the question
and finally the leaving

and it is only then
that the dust can settle
on the road

the river begin
flowing again
under the bridge
and the mountains
return to walking

BEDTIME

Kosho the toad lies down
in his bed at night
and starts relaxing
his muscles one by one
starting with his toes
and proceeding
to the top-most wrinkle
on his skin, but each night
he always seems to skip
over one
or another
in a leg
or in his groin
or his heart
or, most often
the darkest muscle
of muscles, that since
the beginning of time
can never be found
and like the tip
of the ox's tail
stays taut and caught
in the window, unseen
just beyond reach, too
gristly to go through.

UNDOING

After many years
of deep study
and great weariness
of flesh, withering
of eyelids, Kosho
clicks the cap of his pen
onto the barrel, closes
the blurring, moon-
illuminated pages
before him, clears
his throat and shuffles
toward his back door
which, of its own
accord, opens
onto a garden
planted with flowers
and vegetables, herbs
and frail grasses, with slugs
gnawing at low leaves, beetles
chewing and shitting
and dark families of mold
gathering together
and bowing their heads
in prayer, like ink
consuming paper.

ROAD

Kosho walks all day
down a road
like a river
and meets not a single
anyone or anything.

In the evening
he stops, gathers wood
and builds a small fire
to warm himself and roast
his last sweet potato.

All night he sleeps
and in the morning sits
a long time in the cold
until he forgets the way
he came to this place
and where he was trying to go.

This dream he has
many times in both
his sleeping hours
and waking hours
and fills his days
with all the scenery
and all the lives
of all the ones living
on all sides
of the road and traveling
on the road itself.

One Blossom, One Body

Kosho the toad sits
in his boat in the dark
night, the red and green
light in the bow bobs
up and down, up and down
in the chop, the clear
light in the stern rises
and falls, drawing his rod
and his line up and down
through the water, swaying
side to side, the great
heavens above wheeling
and only the pole star
seems not to move
but it is also
speeding away, a cell
in the same great
body, a blossom
in the same spiral
garland of flowers
and Kosho the seed
within the seed.

TEACHINGS

One early summer
evening, Kosho
completely bewildered
and without words
meets God walking
through the garden
pinching back pepper blossoms
that have gotten ahead
of their roots, thinning
the long, cool rows
of greens, plucking
newly formed beetles
from cucumber leaves
and crushing them
lovingly between
almighty finger
and thumb.

ENTERING THE MOUNTAIN

Coming around
to the north-facing slope
Kosho discovers
a crystal tree blooming
in a remnant of snow.

The unfiltered light
of the sun washes
over rocks and crags
and flows down
through glowing leaves
the way dawn explodes
on the surface
of a hidden
and long deserted pond

Kosho sighs and moves
up the canyon
and enters the mountain
with an open heart
following a stream
and sweet music
rising from the water.

WANDERING

Kosho the toad wanders
alone on the mountain
with empty pockets
and laden mind, asking
each tree he passes
the same question
and getting the same answer
from each one

here, a dropped needle

there, a cone half buried
in a bed of needles

a universe of needles

and overhead
the silent branches.

ROCKS, LOGS, LICHENS

Kosho moves slowly
through pine forest
following a shallow
stream flowing with water
that was snow
only minutes before.

All around him rocks
and fallen logs sit
silently, covered
with lichens.

Kosho's eyes are not
open, not closed, his
breath perfectly in time
with rocks, logs, lichens

sun and moon
not one, not two
and the sky
opens in perfect
trackless silence
and slipstreams
left behind by wings.

PURITY

Kosho the toad
like a lion leaves
the mountain
where he has been staying
and moves down through dust
and tinder dry leaves
and grasses along
the coast to a place
where waves crash against the rocks
and surge through caves
worn like shimmering windows
by the winds and tides.

On a sweeping margin
of sand, he finds
the decomposing bodies
of a seal and a rat
the size of a dog
and in the shade
of the trees, a spring
flowing with clear water
so fresh and so pure
that even at night
the moon does not float in it.

Depth

The longer Kosho sits
in the great and empty
depth of night
and the deeper he sinks
the greater his body
and mind grow
until he melts
into the walls of the room
where he is sitting, then
the foundation and footings
of the house, the grass and rocks
outside, roads, fields, fence rows
and sky above, all
the bodies of earth and air
and sea and space, with all
its bodies, the planets
and stars floating there, dark
bodies, shining bodies, dark
matter, the moon shining
in his hand, and then
Kosho sighs
again, returning
and beginning, just one
cell in an empty
universe, then two cells, there
in the great and empty depth.

Dog

Once, Kosho had a sly, fast
dog, all liver-colored
with floppy ears, docked
tail and wild eyes
who slept in the heat
and ran in the cold, chasing
the light of the sun
and the reflection
of the moon, pierced
in the chest by hayrake tines
and feet quilled with locust thorns.

It was only when this dog
was completely dead
and Kosho could let it
run on ahead without him
that he could return, body
and soul together
to the country
where he
and the dog were born.

Nutmeg

Kosho holds the child close
in his arms.

Her blond hair is thin
as an old woman's
and falls down over
her face, covering
her pale blue eyes.

She turns her head back
and forth, as if seeing
the planet around her, again
for the very first time
and every now and then
she shakes the jar of dried
nutmeg seeds she holds
in her hand and Kosho
wakes again
from the deep sleep, barren
dreams and laboring mind
that have burdened his species
since the very
beginning of time.

PENTECOST

After a whole life
spent in study
at midnight
of the longest night
of the year, Kosho
suddenly pushes
to the end of the table
The Bible, Complete
Works of Shakespeare, To Kill
a Mockingbird, Blue Cliff
Record, Phaedrus, Joy
of Sex, Diamond
Sutra, Aristotle's
Rhetoric, Tain, Magna
Carta, Constitution
and the confused *Sayings*
of Layman P'ang, all
the other books
he is reading, all the notes
he has taken, soaks them
with kerosene from the lamp
he has been using
and lights the last match
in the house.

The fire spreads slowly
from small tongues of flame
to a blaze so bright
Kosho wants to get
his sunglasses
and for added protection
spread sunscreen on his face
and the backs of his hands.

TOAD IN THE SNOW

From where he sits
Kosho the toad sees
a single flake of snow
fall through the air
and settle on the ground
between a leaf
and a blade of grass

then another

and another

until all but Kosho's
eyes, ears and nose
are completely
covered and the sky
merges with the ground

and it is only then
that Kosho can just
begin to sense the tiger
moving toward him.

GOLDEN

On a spring day that no words
could ever explain
Kosho is catching one fish
after another.

Some of these fish
he carefully drops
into a deep
bluegreen bucket
full of fresh water
where they turn
into glowing
golden orbs

others, he releases
back to the lake
where they also become
glowing golden orbs

and Kosho becomes
golden as well
in his golden boat
floating on the light chop
on a spring day
like a flower held up
or a spoon
no words
could ever explain.

TRAVELER

From the green valley floor
crisscrossed by streams

through a herd of elk, deer
on the margins

silent coyote passages

sheep gathered together
at rust-colored pools

Kosho the toad hikes up
toward the pass and over
the divide, with just
a stick in his hand, pack
on his back, a coat rolled
and tied on beneath, all
in momentary balance
and what he leaves behind
no one understands
and where he goes, no one
really knows.

One boot is on, the other
lost; the solid ground
melts away
beneath his feet
with each step
and the thin air
and empty sky ahead
is crowded with stars.

RETURNING

Kosho sits at the bar
in front of an empty glass.

In the backbar mirror
he watches two old men
playing gin
in the far corner
near the restroom doors
where an empty bucket
rests on its side.

This game has been going on
for over forty years
yet neither man
has the lead
and neither is behind.

All the other chairs
and stools in the bar
are empty
and the bartender
is gone from behind the bar.

Kosho slides off his stool
and hops out the door.

Down at the pier
the last ferry idles
in deep bluegreen water

golden fish with bones
that glow through their flesh

keep passing through a net
put in place by others
who have also long since gone.

Notes

Most of the poems in Part 2 are based on selected koans taken from the first half of *The Blue Cliff Record*, a collection of public cases compiled and annotated by Chinese Zen Masters in the ninth, tenth, and eleventh centuries.

The concluding lines of "Edge" are taken from Hunter S. Thompson's *Hell's Angels: The Strange and Terrible Saga of the Outlaw Motorcycle Gangs*. The situation depicted in the poem is taken from Shohaku Okumura's *Living by Vow*.

The lines in the Interlink are patterned after the lines in the text accompanying the Oxherding Pictures by Kuo-an Shihyuan. The source I drew them from is Philip Kapleau's *Three Pillars of* Zen.

The italicized lines in "The Holy Truths Are Empty" are adapted from the *Blue Cliff Record*.

The italicized lines in "Cakes" are taken from the *Blue Cliff Record*.

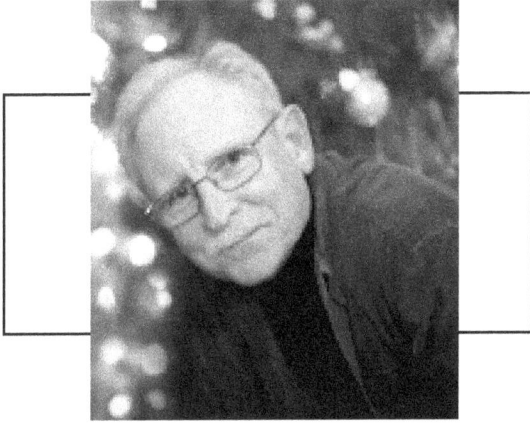

Robert Tremmel grew up in Northwest Iowa and went to the University of Iowa. After hauling furniture and teaching high school for a few years, he went back to Iowa as a graduate student, taught seven years at Washburn University in Topeka, Kansas, and then finished out his teaching career at Iowa State University. In 1992, along with three others, he co-founded the Des Moines Zen Center, and has practiced there ever since. He has published widely as both an English educator and a poet, and is the author of three books of poetry as well as *Zen and the Practice of Teaching English*. He and his wife Michelle live in Ankeny, Iowa.

Books in the Laughing Buddha Series

The Records of Kosho the Toad by Robert Tremmel

Ohio Zen Poems: All the Difference by d. steven conkle
and *Inside the Garden* by Larry Smith

Chinese Zen Poems: What Hold Has this Mountain,
translated by Mei Hui Liu Huang and Larry Smith

*Songs of the Woodcutter: Zen Poems of Wang Wei &
Taigu Ryokan*, translated by Mei Hui Liu Huang and
Larry Smith with flute by Monte Page (CD and booklet)

America Zen: A Gathering of Poets, (anthology)
eds. Larry Smith and Ray McNiece

The Kanshi Poems of Taigu Ryokan, translated by
Mei Hui Liu Huang and Larry Smith

Each Moment All: Poems by Larry Smith

Tu Fu Comes to America: A Story in Poems
by Larry Smith

Bottom Dog Press
http//smithdocs.net

www.ingramcontent.com/pod-product-compliance
Lightning Source LLC
Chambersburg PA
CBHW031145090426
42738CB00008B/1232